Lands of the Cathars

Lands of

Gérard Sioen

MENGÈS

LE PAYS CATHARE

the Cathars

text by Henri Gougaud

with the collaboration of
Jean-Michel Leniaud for the legends

LE PAYS CATHARE

Faced with the necessary restructuring of its economy and with the new exigencies imposed by decentralization, the land of the Cathars affirms that consideration of its medieval heritage is a matter of priority because of the capacity of that heritage to generate a new economy. The *Conseils généraux* of the Ariège, Aude and Hérault *départements* have drawn up an amenity plan for their territories in which the medieval history of the south provides the mainspring of development, a source of cultural and economic enrichment. This political decision, embarked on resolutely in 1990, was stimulated by awareness not only of the cultural heritage of each of the three *départements* but also of the fame of the Cathar phenomenon in France and throughout Europe. Studies of attendance and awareness carried out in the last few years confirm the growing interest, which you share, in experiencing sites and spaces that bear the imprint of a story that exists at the highest level of humanity, of faith and of passion. To respond to this strong desire for authenticity, emotion and accuracy, from the outset there could be no question of rushing into action meaninglessly, without careful thought about the heritage of the past and the treatment that it demands in the present, without respect for cultural authenticity, for truth and for honesty in relation to history. To guarantee the existence and long life of a development programme based on the exploitation of our heritage, it is necessary to privilege historic truth supported by research, to privilege quality in the respect shown for visitors. A region of which the national memory has forgotten, or scarcely remembers, or misremembers a religion which was one of the finest messages of salvation derived from Christianity has decided, centuries later, to revive a part of its history that goes well beyond the all-too-famous "Albigensian Crusade". The memory of that period is thus to be rediscovered and restored. It is to this rediscovery that we invite you now. The land of the Cathars uses rehabilitated memory as process, reconstructed memory as material... You are the actors, and this work is a magnificent key to discovery.

I.S.B.N.: 2-8562-0347-7
© Éditions Mengès, Paris, 1992.
© English version, Éditions Mengès, Paris, 1994.
6, rue du Mail, 75002 Paris, France.
Dépôt légal: avril 1994
Printed in Italy by Grafiche Lema

ACKNOWLEDGMENTS

We would like to thank the Conseil Général de l'Aude, the Centre National d'Etudes Cathares and the Comité Départemental du Patrimoine Audois for their help during the preparation of this work.

The land of the Corbières is poor, thorny, deserted, but welcoming to those in search of memory. Everything here is thin, stripped down to essentials. There are doors in ragged walls which seem to invite one into another realm that is familiar, peaceful, indifferent to the turmoil of the world. It is a land which has become wise through suffering. Step confidently forward on its paths and you will savour the taste of knowledge that is captivating but impossible to define.

The Romans first occupied this region, and left traces of their presence. The Visigoths too. Spain is not far away. The Mediterranean is on the doorstep. Toulouse smells of spices. In Narbonne, that Roman city, Jewish scholars founded one of the most famous schools of their time, where they taught grammar and elaborated commentaries on the Kabbalah. The Arabs joined in this concert of learning, contributing poetry, algebra and architecture. Here they spoke *occitan*, like Dante, feeding on the strange and revolutionary work of a few men from who knows where - the troubadours.

The troubadours appeared at the beginning of the thirteenth century, bearers of a gift beyond price: the heart's fire, love, woman fully alive at last. Before them, the question was still asked whether these half-men had souls; and the answer given was often in the negative. A woman could be a mother, a servant or a whore, creature of the devil or comforter of the warrior; but a true companion of the heart ? The troubadours discovered woman, sang of her, and changed the world. It became a little gentler, a little more elevated, dreamed of something greater than itself. Suddenly it was said that the love of a woman was a gift of grace, and that the exaltation of the soul sparked by such love was the only thing capable of freeing man from the narrow boundaries of the self. People spoke of joy and honour in love. They "talked fine", waged poetic war, and wrote to one another in verse.

This was the time when the count of Toulouse chose a poor knight, Raymond de Miraval, as his closest friend, because the knight was a great poet. It was the time when Bernard de Ventadour, in the suite of Eleanor of Aquitaine, carried courtly love and the *occitan* language to the court of England. It was the time when Jaufré Rudel sang of a distant love, "the unattainable star". The time, finally, when Peire Vidal, out of devotion for the Lady of Pennautier known as the She-Wolf, withdrew into the forest, clad only in a wolf's skin. The legend is revealing: we are told that the shepherds, taking him for a real wolf, roughed him up and delivered him in a sorry state to the castle of Pennautier, where "the She-Wolf and her husband received him with great amusement. And the husband, who was not of a jealous disposition but was a man of honour, had him taken to a quiet place and did all that he could for him. He sent for a doctor and had him cared for until he was well again."

It is difficult today to realize just how novel such sentiments were in the thirteenth century. Until these poets found voice, companionship of the heart was a strictly masculine affair. There was brotherhood, especially brotherhood in arms. Two knights might swear eternal friendship and strict fidelity. To seal their commitment, they made a cut in their wrists and mingled their blood. Symbolically by doing this they mingled their souls, which became a single soul occupying two bodies. This fraternal bond, what we call blood-brotherhood, was known as *affrèrement*.

The troubadours were the first who dared consider that women were worthy of this kinship of the soul. They did not call for an exchange of blood, judging it perhaps too savage. Instead they went one better: they invented the kiss on the mouth between man and woman - an exchange of breath that was a mutual engagement as solemn and sacred as the exchange of blood between brothers in arms.

Here was something to worry churchmen. It wouldn't take much to make them regard these men as emissaries of the Devil. What the troubadours spread, to the tunes of the time, was a sense of irrepressible liberty.

They did not fall silent, but were still there when the age of savagery set in. For among the eccentric southerners there were not only men who were love-mad: there were people who were God-mad - the heretics who followed the Cathar faith.

Their story began in the tenth century and gained momentum in the twelfth, when merchants, pedlars, and learned travellers came from Central Europe bringing with them a new religion: the faith of the *patarins*, *purs*

(pure) or *boni homines* (good men), who were to become known as "Cathars". They were Christians, but of a curious persuasion. For them, the world was created by Satan, the fallen angel. Is it not the case that our earth, our towns, villages, churches, hierarchies, bodies, loves, are perishable ? The fact is undeniable. But God, who is eternal and unchanging, cannot create anything that is not itself eternal and unchanging. Good, in the sense in which that word was understood at the time, is that which comes from God: an eternal flame enclosed within living creatures. Evil is that which cannot last, but must yield to the ravages of time: matter. We are moulded out of a mixture of eternity and matter. And our task here on earth is to separate out within ourselves the good seed from the dross, the divine flame that shall be free from the case in which it is imprisoned, a husk whose fate is oblivion. Such a task cannot be accomplished in a single lifetime; it can only be achieved through many reincarnations.

This belief was not new. The Early Christians held it for a time. However, it became coloured by an attitude of contempt for the world so subversive as to alarm authorities of all kinds. To those indifferent to the things of this world, property rights and feudal duties meant nothing. Furthermore, since all flesh was created by the Devil, there was no fundamental difference between the union of bodies in the marriage bed and chance encounters. In either case, it was self-evident that procreation must be avoided as much as possible, since to give birth to a child is to fetter a divine spark in the prison of matter, to condemn an innocent soul to the fire of the suffering in which we struggle with no prospect but death. New lives are, nevertheless, necessary: how else would reincarnation be possible ? Christ did indeed come to succour mankind, but he did not become flesh. He only had the appearance of a body. Thus he did not suffer on the cross. If the Cathars felt horror at the sight of the cross, that was only because it was a symbolic proof of the wickedness of the world. "When I see a cross, I spit", said the *purs*. "If some bandit broke your father's skull with a cudgel, would you love that cudgel ? Would you genuflect before it and kiss it with devotion ?"

The men who spoke thus were for the most part educated, trained in the arena of public debates or disputations. Yet nothing marked them off from the common run. Their clothes were like anyone else's, and they did not enjoy any special privileges. They moved among the people like a fish in water. They earned their living like the rest, most of them as craftsmen or merchants. The Catholic Church, for its part, had coffers bulging with gold, owned serfs, and levied taxes. How could one believe her bishops, with their fingers laden with rings, their fat bellies and their princely palaces, when they preached the poverty commended in the Gospels ? They inspired a silent revolt, all the more hate-filled because it could not be voiced. And the *purs* were listened to all the more intently because they preached not under the sounding vaults of cathedrals but in public squares and outside village churches, which no one now attended. In 1198 the situation was such that Pope Innocent III, disturbed by the progress of this heresy in the Midi, invented the Inquisition, and issued an order "to the princes, counts, and all the barons and great men in their provinces to give all the assistance in their power to his envoys against the heretics; to proscribe those whom Brother Guy will have excommunicated, to confiscate their possessions and to use even greater rigour against them if they should persist in wanting to remain in the land after their excommunication."

These measures remained ineffective. The influence of the *boni homines* increased daily. As a writer, I like to recall the texts in their favour:

> While worthlessness ascends to the heights,
> I see the fall of valour and of noble birth;
> I see the treacherous admonishing the good,
> honest people preached to by thieves,
> those who have strayed pointing the way to the wise.

Thus Peire Cardenal. And here is Guilhem Figuera, in a famous, fierce song:

> Rome, fools are meat for your festivities,
> you lead the blind straight into the ditch,
> selling teachings of God to make yourself rich,

and your heart so venal
for a *sou* of metal
will absolve all sins. Rome, you are gravid
with a great burden of ill.

In 1207 the papal legate, Pierre de Castelnau, passed judgment on Raymond, count of Toulouse, sixth of the name, and found him guilty of excessive leniency towards the heretics. It is a fact that in his castle Raymond retained both a Catholic confessor and two spiritual advisers who were notoriously associated with heresy. He was excommunicated, found that unacceptable, and ordered the assassination of the ill-advised legate who had been so presumptuous as to pronounce sentence against him. In retaliation for this murder, the pope declared a crusade against a land which, according to contemporary chroniclers, had fallen back into the worst aberrations of paganism. In 1209 the largest army anyone could remember burst upon the Languedoc, led by the boldest barons of France under the spiritual leadership of Arnaud Amaury, abbot of Cîteaux.

The first city to suffer siege was Béziers. The abbot charged all good Catholics to come out, or else be mown down with the heretical weeds that he had come to destroy. Only six Jews, reluctant to be caught between the hammer and the anvil, emerged. Béziers was taken and sacked. In the words of the *Chanson de la croisade albigeoise* (Song of the Albigensian Crusade), "They were all killed, since nothing worse could be done[1]". Two weeks later Carcassonne surrendered, almost without a fight. Its young viscount, Raymond-Roger Trencavel, was thrown into prison where he died, ostensibly of dysentery but probably poisoned. Rule over the conquered land was entrusted to Simon de Montfort.

Simon de Montfort - an implacable strategist, a saint fully as much as an executioner, hated more than a devil and yet an enigma. What a fate was his ! He had come on crusade after opening his Psalter at random in search of a sign from God: he found it, and immediately took up arms. His selection as leader came after Carcassonne had been captured through a notorious act of treachery. Trencavel, the impetuous viscount, just twenty years old, had left the safety of his walls alone and unarmed, to negotiate an honourable settlement. Instead of being received, he was taken prisoner - a particularly disgraceful action at a time when honour was deemed the greatest virtue. At that the people of Carcassonne lost heart and, according to legend, they all fled in the night through underground passages. The crusaders had won without a massacre, but also without glory. It was then that abbot of Cîteaux decided to appoint a commander-in-chief for his army. The most powerful lords among the crusaders declined; Simon de Montfort accepted. Was it the ambitious act of a rough professional soldier short of funds, as has been said ? Yet Simon was not a landless knight: through his mother he was earl of Leicester, and through his wife Alix he was related to the king of France, who had placed him in charge of the forests of Ile-de-France. And far from having voracious appetites, he was austere, chaste, even devout. His lady was the Virgin, and to her he dedicated his battles. Finally, to have overall military responsibility for the crusade was a burden rather than an honour. That, perhaps, rather than moral scruple, is why the highest-ranking barons left the task to this man who is so hard to visualize, even though we have the word of his contemporary admirer Pierre des Vaux-de-Cernay, author of the *Historia albigensis*, that he was tall, elegant in his person, and of pleasant expression, "alert and lively in his bearing - in short, full of grace in all respects[2]".

Simon thus took up residence in the citadel with a few brave and faithful lieutenants. He had no time to relax. Throughout the region, resistance was getting organized. The Corbières mountains bristled with castles as inaccessible as eagle's nests, whose inhabitants were used to the loneliness of the heights and feared neither God nor the Devil. Here the hunted heretics found refuge. The castle-dwellers looked down on the valleys below where the crusader armies floundered in the stony scrubland, and jeered.

A day's march from Carcassonne stood the three castles of Lastours, each crowning a rocky crag: Quertinheux, Cabaret and Fleur-Espine. Pierre-Roger de Cabaret, former *viguier* or deputy ruler of Carcassonne, and his brother Jourdain sheltered within their walls several *faidits* (southern lords dispossessed by the conquest) and a handful of heretics. Simon de Montfort led his troops to the foot of the towers and gave the order to attack. The enterprise was totally senseless, as he soon realized: on these hostile slopes he risked losing the best of his men in return for a doubtful gain. He raised the siege. In the strongholds above there was jubilation; but it was misguided. The defenders did not know that Simon de Montfort was the most stubborn, unbending, and perhaps fundamentally the most insane of men. In March 1211, the inhabitants of Cabaret saw on the mountain path leading up to the castle a pathetic group of some hundred wandering souls, whose faces were bleeding wounds: their eyes had been put out, their noses and ears cut off. One only had been left an eye, to serve as their guide. Simon had just captured the castle of Bram in the Lauragais. He had ordered these atrocities in the conquered town and dispatched this nightmare band with the sole purpose of terrorizing the defenders of Cabaret. The message was understood. During an earlier skirmish, Pierre-Roger had captured one of Simon's close lieutenants, Bouchard de Marly; now he freed him from the dungeon where he had been held, gave him his finest horse, and surrendered to him his own person, his castles and his lands.

Simon de Montfort was gracious to those who yielded. He offered Pierre-Roger a new estate, on condition that he would lead a quiet life there - but the latter preferred exile in Roussillon, where he died ten years later. Faced with the storm that had struck them, many of the southern nobles followed him in surrendering to Simon, and went over to the crusading army. Their heart was not in it, however: they submitted because they had no other choice, but they grumbled and looked for the first opportunity to go back on their word and use their arms on the other side. They have been called fickle, but whereas for Simon de Montfort to go back on your word was the greatest possible dishonour, for those who had given their word under duress it was perhaps the only way to return to life.

There were some, however, who refused to submit, even in show. One of those was Guillaume de Minerve - a leading figure among the knights of the time, a friend of troubadours, who sang the beauty of his wife, and a covert protector of Cathars. His castle of Minerve stood at the top of a great precipice overlooking the dry riverbed of a tributary of the Aude, and was, according to Pierre des Vaux-de-Cernay, "so strong it could scarce be believed[2]". Montfort set siege to it in 1210 at the beginning of a particularly hot summer. Guillaume was not worried: he had a thousand defenders, and was not a man to be impressed by the fall of Carcassonne and the surrender of Cabaret. Simon arrived below his walls with a battery of military engines and plentiful troops, and encircled the stronghold. "To the west", reports the chronicler, "a mangonel was in action day and night." Skirmishes and attacks left corpses everywhere to corrupt the blazing heat of summer. Minerve soon began to run out of water, then of food, until to the constant scraping sound of cicadas it had become a furnace where you could not even breathe. The stern Guillaume realized that negotiation was imperative. He would yield, he told Simon, on condition that the lives of the heretics he had sheltered would be spared. "Agreed", said Simon, "on condition that they renounce their false beliefs and accept the authority of the Church." Some of his followers found this too soft. "Do not be anxious", said Arnaud Amaury, the papal legate: "I think very few will convert." His cynicism proved justified. "On 22 July the crusaders took possession of Minerve. At the head of the procession was the cross, followed by Simon de Montfort's banners. All sang the *Te Deum* and marched to the church. Once it had been purified, they placed the cross at the top of the tower and distributed Simon's banners elsewhere. Christ had taken the town, and it was fitting that his ensign should take first place, displayed at the highest point."

The heretics had gathered in a house in the village, where they awaited the arrival of the abbot of Vaux-de-Cernay. They did not have to wait long. The great cleric addressed them in pressing and almost certainly sincere terms, entreating them to renounce their faith. Not one replied. He promised that their lives would be spared. The only answer was a murmur of prayer. One hundred and forty heretics perished in a single enormous bonfire. Guillaume de Minerve abandoned his castle, and presented himself and all his possessions to the Knights Hospitallers of St John of Jerusalem. He is mentioned again a few years later at the siege of Beaucaire, where, according to the author of the *Chanson de la croisade*, he fought "like a demon[1]". After that we lose sight of him.

Once Minerve had been subdued, without a moment's rest the ogre Simon de Montfort marched on Termes, in the heart of the Corbières. His knights followed, but then lost their nerve and protested. The tracks amid the rocks and scrub could scarcely be made out, and at any moment they might be attacked by one of the savage bands known to haunt these sun-baked labyrinths. Simon tirelessly revived their faith and their courage: "God marches before us. Who could have a better guide ? He will lead us to success." They reached Termes at last without too much difficulty, but here the men were at once faced with further challenges. The castle stood on a sheer mountaintop, surrounded by ravines: to reach it, they would have to descend to the bottom of these gullies, filled with impenetrable scrub, and then they would have to crawl up to the heights through rocks and clumps of box, risking their neck at every step.

The lord of this land, Raymond de Termes, wearing a golden helmet, looked down on the crusaders from the top of his wall. He was a proud and energetic man. The attack had long been expected, and he was amply supplied with provisions and with men prepared for anything. Among the many *faidits* who had sought refuge with him was Guillaume de Roquefort, one of the most powerful landowners of the Montagne Noire and now a redoubtable guerrilla fighter; a year earlier, he had risked himself as far as the walls of Carcassonne to assassinate several priests.

Simon, on the other hand, was short of men. He was expecting reinforcements from Brittany, Saxony, Bavaria, Normandy, Lombardy, the German lands, and of course from Ile-de-France, but they were slow in arriving. This, it proved, was because the people of Cabaret were always out on the roads, attacking supply convoys, destroying the war machines painstakingly dismantled and carried in pieces over the mountain tracks, and sending Simon's men on in mutilated condition. During all this time, according to Pierre des Vaux-de-Cernay, the people in the castle "looked down from the ramparts and taunted the crusaders, came out to fetch water and returned unmolested", and hunted down like hares the scrawny troops who ventured among the rocks and the bristling *maquis* of their mountain.

The reinforcements did, however, arrive, little by little. The war machines were finally erected and started to bombard the walls. The siege began in earnest at the height of August, and soon became bogged down. The fierce dry summer dragged out, as it can in this part of France, until late October. There had been no rain for three months. And for the people of the castle, with their cisterns now empty, there was no other source of water. The crusaders lacked food, but they had plenty of streams. Raymond de Termes was the first to yield: he came down from his mountain, stood before Simon de Montfort, and offered him the keys of the castle on condition that they would be returned to him after a suitable few months' penitence. Simon accepted - showing that he no longer believed he could win by force, if he ever had.

That very evening, the sky put an end to this inglorious peace. A spectacular storm broke over the country, sending waterfalls cascading down the slopes and filling the cisterns to overflowing. For Raymond de Termes, it was a sign that God was on the side of the besieged, and he decided to resume the struggle. Simon's emissaries, come to receive his submission, were greeted with arrows and stones. Tired, dispirited and short of food, the crusaders after this stroke of fate had only one desire: to quit this remote world's end and return to their moist Edens in the Ile-de-France, for which they were bitterly homesick. The bishops of Chartres and Beauvais, the counts of Dreux and Ponthieu, "and a great many other noble figures" left the camp, Pierre des Vaux-de-Cernay tells us, "overwhelmed by a desire to return home". Simon hesitated. He prayed ceaselessly, asking God for guidance. On 21 November, "he worked all day on his plans, and fasted". At nightfall he withdrew to his tent, having decided that at dawn the next day he would attack the castle with what troops remained.

On 22 November, after sixteen weeks of siege, his men reached the walls with ropes, defying vertigo - and found the citadel empty. Raymond de Termes had been wrong: God had indeed made a choice between the combatants, but his camp had not been chosen. The bodies of rats that had perished in the empty cisterns had contaminated the water of that long-hoped-for deluge, and the thirsty defenders, seized with colic, had fled, apparently through underground passages in the heart of the mountain. Through these narrow tunnels by torchlight Simon's men pursued them, caught them, massacred those who resisted and took prisoner those who were too frightened to react. Raymond was brought in chains in a cart to Carcassonne, where he died three years later, forgotten, in a stinking dungeon.

After Termes, the indomitable Simon set his sights on Puivert, which came to him easily. Puivert later became the residence of the Bruyères family and the most pleasant castle in the region, nestling amid trees on the lower slopes leading up to the heights of the Ariège. Many texts mention it as a meeting-place of troubadours, who came to do combat in verse, and it continued to welcome music, as we can see today in one of the rooms of the keep, where corbels still in almost perfect condition show musicians playing the psaltery, lute, viol, tambourine, bagpipes, portative organ, gittern and rebec.

Over the next few years, with the blessing of the papal legate, Simon de Montfort ravaged the province of Toulouse and the area around Foix, pressed forward as far as Provence, was checked at Beaucaire, and returned again finally to Languedoc. The Lateran Council in 1215 made him the new count of Toulouse. Raymond VI, however, after two years in exile, had resumed residence within the walls and was waiting for him there. Simon laid siege to the city. It was to be his last battle. Below the ramparts of Toulouse, nine months into the siege, on the feast day of John the Baptist (24 June) 1218 he died, his head shattered by a stone fired from one of a battery of machines manoeuvred by women on the wall-top. News of his death was greeted with enthusiasm throughout the south. "Joy spread at once throughout the streets", says the author of the *Chanson de la croisade*. "People rushed to the churches, lit candles, offered up a thousand thanks, and sang out "Vivat ! my lord of Montfort is no more ! that murderer, that bandit who caused us so much suffering has died unshriven !" The sound of horns, bugles and trumpets mingled joyfully with the ringing of bells, the jingling of tambourines and the beating of kettledrums, and people laughed as they danced in the paved squares." Simon's body was solemnly buried in the cathedral of Saint-Nazaire in Carcassonne. The same anonymous troubadour who gave us an account of his death bade him farewell in a pitiless epitaph:

On his tombstone it is clearly engraved
that he was a saint and martyr, and will rise again,
that he will know the perfect joy of the Elect,
and will wear a crown at the right hand of God.
Will it be so ? Perhaps in truth it will.
If by slaughtering men and spilling blood,
by torturing souls and preaching massacres,
by leaving the true path and debasing the name of Honour,
by plundering the land, by exalting Pride,
by enflaming evil, and extinguishing good,
by massacring women with their babes at their breast,
one can on this earth conquer Jesus Christ,
then Sir Simon will sit, resplendent, in Heaven !

The southerners for a time believed they had won. That was without reckoning on the obstinacy of the Church. Pope Honorius III preached a new crusade, and in 1219 an entirely new army, led by Louis, eldest son of the king of France, descended on the Midi. War resumed. Between massacres and moments of hope, councils and debates, it moved on to its inexorable end. In 1231 the first tribunal of the Inquisition sat in Carcassonne. In 1240, the rebellious *faidits* were crushed by the French barons. Then the last strongholds on the southern edge of the Corbières fell, among them Peyrepertuse. Seeing its ruins today, almost indistinguishable from the rock on which they sit, you wonder how one side could possibly have fought their way up so high, and why the other fought so hard to defend this gateway to the sky. In fact, three days of siege sufficed to reduce it. Its defenders, it seems, no longer nourished any hope on earth or in heaven. The war that had gone on relentlessly for thirty years had worn down everything, undone everything, crushed souls perhaps even more violently than physical walls. The country clearly had no future. At last came the *coup de grâce*, at Montségur.

Ever since Raymond de Péreille had made over the citadel to the Cathar Church, a few men and women *Perfecti* ("perfect ones", or "initiates") had dwelt there, as peacefully as in the hand of God, out of reach of the fury of princes, the fulmination of priests, and the thousand troubles of the age. Everywhere but on this mountain there was nothing but plague in the soul and fear of being burned alive. The noblemen of Béziers, Foix, Provence and Comminges gave their daughters in marriage to the Frenchmen, extended begging bowls to the pope, and spat at one another in the bitterness of defeat. Between secret heresy and terror of the rough soldiers and the Dominicans, the populace gradually sank into despair. In their hearts, they were ashamed of living in worse servitude than dogs.

Montségur alone stood apart from these griefs. It occupied a site so high, guarded by such deep and wild ravines, that not one of the barons of the Roman Church had throughout the years dared to risk his life below its walls. Yet the forces there were minimal: scarcely more than a hundred soldiers, squires, and landless knights joined in the routines of the dormitory, the lookouts on the wall-walks, and the upkeep of harnesses, weapons and defensive ramparts.

In October 1243, when the wagons, standards, horsemen and foot-soldiers of the last crusade appeared on the road down in the valley, it seemed that a whole town full of people had burst on a land that had known nothing but the furtive wild animals of the mountains. Over a period of four days, numberless canvas hamlets were erected, their pointed roofs bright with banners. The people of Montségur scarcely took notice. They felt that no one could possibly dislodge them - the more so since Raymond VII, the young count of Toulouse, still uncertain whether to rebel or submit, had promised them his support. For a long time during the siege visitors and peasants continued to come and go out of Montségur, indicating that the mountain was impossible to encircle.

It was not until a troop of Gascon mercenaries climbed the cliff-face to the east in the middle of the night, in the depth of December, that the belief that they could go on resisting for ever collapsed at a stroke. Surely no living being, unless he had wings, could climb such a height. Yet these bold men had, an hour before dawn, reached the topmost part of the summit. There, opposite the abyss, stood a tower separated from the castle by a strip of rough ground where a path ran between bushes and potholes. Once that tower had been taken, it was only a matter of time before the citadel would fall. It held out until 16 March 1244. Not one of the men and women who surrendered that day to the crusaders agreed to renounce their faith; they had no thought of saving their lives. More than two hundred were consigned to the flames. For the survivors, how could it be anything but confirmation of their belief that the world was the creation of the Devil ?

Suffering, malice, torture and intolerance had overcome men and women whose only weapon was the word and whose only thirst was for God. They had gone to meet the Father of Virtuous Spirits (as they called God) through the only door commensurate with their faith - that of fire. The rest, after the burning, took refuge at Puilaurens and Quéribus.

Chabert de Barbaira ruled over those two fortresses. All that is known is that he surrendered them without a struggle, and fled to Barcelona. Once these last islands of resistance had been taken, the hunt for heretics became a matter of, as it were, police work. For Catharism, now an underground movement, held out for a long time with the connivance of the people. Believers were pursued with a relentlessness that seems strange; but the Church had been afraid of being completely superseded, and its cruelty matched its past fears.

The heretics were killed to the very last man. We must imagine these wandering evangelists, after the fall of the final strongholds, travelling the local paths by night, preaching in a low voice around a candle in humble houses which were carefully shuttered and guarded by a reliable friend keeping watch at the door. After the crusade had finished its work, the Inquisition passed judgment on entire villages, hired spies and bounty-hunters, and forced children to betray their fathers and mothers.

A few strangely moving figures stand out among the *Perfecti* of the last days. Pierre Authier was a notary, and a family man. The Inquisition record of the bishop of Pamiers[3] tells us that one day, seated outside his door, he read a passage from St John's Gospel to his brother Guillaume, and asked him: "What do you think, brother ?" His brother replied, "I think we have lost our souls." "Let us leave, then", said Pierre, "and set out to find the salvation of our souls." Straightaway they abandoned all their possessions and travelled to Lombardy, where they were consecrated as *Perfecti*. Pierre, before he was arrested by the Inquisition, preached for a long time in the villages of the Corbières. It was said of him that his word was gold. Until the last flames of the pyre had died down, it seemed that the people might rise to save him.

Amiel de Perles was also arrested, and taken in chains before the Inquisition in Toulouse, where he remained silent in front of the judges. For a month he refused to eat; then, barely able to stand, he was brought face-to-face with Pierre Authier. In the presence of the Inquisitor, the two men only exchanged the ritual adoration. Amiel de Perles was burnt the same day.

The memory of Pons de Châteauverdun survives through a few simple words that stand out from the jumble of the Inquisition records. The last martyr was Guillaume Bélibaste. When in 1305 he found himself wandering lost on the path to a dubious perfection, the faith of the *boni homines* in the lands of the archbishop of Narbonne and the count of Foix was reduced to a few exhausted stragglers. Bélibaste had been a shepherd at

Cubières in the Aude. In an unlucky fit of anger, he killed a man who was threatening to betray his family to the Inquisition. On the very evening of the murder he was visited by Philippe d'Alayrac, a companion of the Authier brothers, and confessed. In the course of the night Philippe managed to convince Bélibaste to follow him on the road to redemption. He led him to the province of Toulouse and made him one of the *Perfecti*. Both men were arrested and taken to prison at Carcassonne, from which they escaped and fled to Catalonia. Philippe then returned alone to Toulouse, where he was caught and burnt at the stake. Deprived of the master who had kept him on the right path, Bélibaste began to feel God seeping out through holes in his soul. He fell in love with a woman, made her pregnant, and then married her off to his best friend; he lost all honour and honesty. And yet, as reluctantly but unswervingly as a blind donkey, he never ceased to walk towards the light of his own revelation. He was brought back to the Ariège by one of those bounty-hunters that the Inquisitors, in this time of sordid persecution, had sent out after the last of the major heretics. Seized on the threshold of death by a kind of madness of love, up to the very end Guillaume kept trying to convert the spy who had sold him. All in vain. The voice of the *Perfecti* was silenced for ever below the castle of Villerouge-Termenès, at the stake where Guillaume Bélibaste perished. Of those long-vanished times there remains nothing now but ruins swept by the murmur of the wind. I imagine that only soft everyday sounds are the same as those which the wandering mystics heard then - the creaking of carts, the cries of shepherds far off, the sound of goat bells, the buzzing of bees, the song of birds. Through this fragile music, through the colours of the sky, and through the lush profusion of growth in the scrublands, you can undertake a never-ending journey into the memory of this land. Rare are the places that possess so little, yet offer so much.

Henri GOUGAUD

1. *La Chanson de la croisade albigeoise*, adapted by Henri Gougaud (Paris: Le Livre de Poche, 1989).
2. Pierre des VAUX-DE-CERNAY, *Historia albigensis*, French translation by Pascal Guébin and Henri Maisonneuve (Paris: Librairie Philosophique J. Vrin, 1951).
3. Jacques Fournier, Bishop of Pamiers (1318-25), *Le Registre d'inquisition de Jacques Fournier*, éd. Jean Duvernoy (Paris/The Hague/New York: Mouton, 1965)

On the following pages, the texts framed within rules are by Jean-Michel Leniaud.

The land
of the Cathars

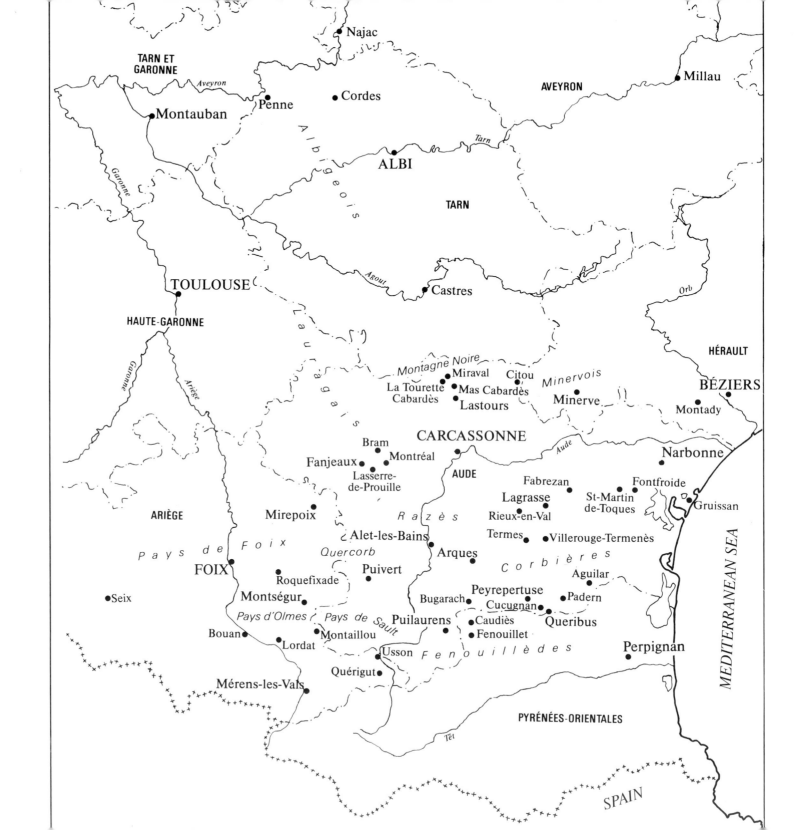

The Pic de Bugarach
Looming like the moon, like a whirling stone sun, the peak is enveloped in magic clouds filled with souls, glowing with light.

23

The present castle of Puivert dates mainly from the fourteenth century. The castle which the troops of Simon de Montfort besieged, under the leadership of Thomas-Pons de Bruyères, was on a slightly different site, and has almost entirely disappeared. Standing at the edge of the Ariège region, the fortress guarded the road between Foix and Perpignan.

ON THE PRECEDING PAGES

1. The Pic de Bugarach, in the south-western part of the Corbières range,
   reaches a height of 1, 231 metres.

2. The Corbières at dawn, seen from the Pic de Bugarach.
   In the distance rise the Pyrenees.

3-8. The castle of Puivert.

Puivert

According to legend, this is where some of the greatest troubadours of the land came to hold a court of love. Time has silenced their voices. The crusade swept across this peaceful country. What remains are the songs of birds in the eternal wild grasses and these upright walls where love poems and war cries seem together to have given birth to nothing but peace.

H.G.

The couverts of Mirepoix

Three faces that are three aspects of the passage of time, carved three times over by the elements and by the hand of man, three reminders to us that we are mortal and that there is no such thing as a new century or a new light.

9

 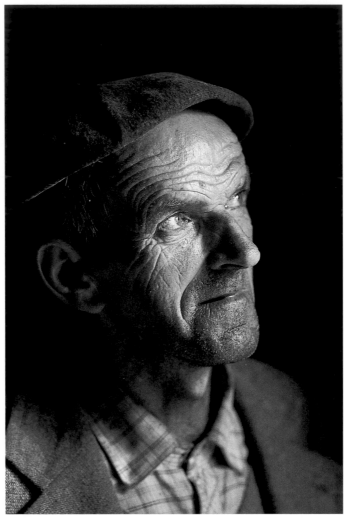

14 15 16

The Corbières

Here there were belongings, stables, doors so thick
they'd taken fifty years of the life of a tree.
There were barrels from which wine seeped out
at the four corners of the courtyard
where paving stones were being laid
with great strokes of the mallet
under the great strokes of the sun.
There was the sound of work,
the scent of everything alive,
bread and meat,
the cries of children,
the splashing of water in the vats.
Then men at the ends of their lives
climbed up the staircases
and vanished beyond the clouds…

(…) H.G.

Foix

The square north tower stands higher than all the rest above the ramparts of Foix. Raymond-Roger, grand protector of heretics, kept it unscathed throughout the whole crusade: Simon de Montfort could do no more than shake his fist at these impassive walls.
H.G.

Spoulga de Bouan

There is nothing cosy or domestic about these walls. A monstrous Cyclops - Bouan, surely - should loom out of the darkness, driving his giant sheep before him, and shading his one eye with his hand against the dazzling light.

Montaillou

Reader, I suggest a game: look at the photograph on the left and shut your eyes, then open them in front of the photograph on the right. There is not a soul left, not even you. In the Pays d'Alion, all that is not stone is light.

Roquefixade

A still point in the world. Here the wind is for ever erasing from the stones what time writes wordlessly with its vast blind force. The castle kneels before the light springing up from behind the mountain.

19 20

23 24

29 30

31 32

After the Council of Toulouse (1229) and the Treaty of Meaux between the count of Toulouse and the king of France (1231), Montségur became the principal stronghold of the Cathars. This eagle's nest, perched at a height of 1, 207 metres, lay in the lands of Guy de Lévis. The castle proper was restored from 1204 onwards and became the centre of an important pilgrimage and market. The Cathars did not live within the fortress, which was too small, but in houses corbelled out on the mountainside or clustered in a village at the foot. Some came to this holy place only when they were dying, to receive the final sacrament or consolamentum. In 1232 the Cathar bishop Guilhabert de Castres asked the feudal lord, Raymond de Perella (or Péreille), to make his castle the official seat of what remained of the Cathar Church. Raymond VII, count of Toulouse, made several halfhearted attempts to capture it; finally in 1241 he promised Louis IX - the future St Louis - that he would destroy this pocket of resistance.

In 1243 Montségur successfully resisted a five-month siege. Not until the appearance of a great war machine, installed under conditions of great difficulty at the beginning of the winter in order to bombard the defenders, did the Cathars' furious resolve begin to weaken. Durandus, bishop of Albi, served as engineer for this operation. The barbican was then invested, and the Cathars carried their treasure away into safekeeping, but the castle still held out. Finally on 14 March 1244, after the celebration of the Cathar Easter, the citadel surrendered and all the inhabitants were burnt alive.

It had been a ruin that the Lord of Péreille had restored, and later presented to the hounded Cathars. It was a ruin that the crusaders left after the great bonfire of 1244. They rebuilt the castle, and it is their ruin that clings today to the shoulder of the mountain, as if desperately reaching towards that heaven that welcomed two hundred Perfecti on a single terrible day.

H.G.

House of rock
house kneaded out of blood and sun
house as remote as the souls of the dead
unattainable cradle
both bird and ship
house with walls made of petrified sky -
Montségur.

H.G.

ON THE PRECEDING PAGES

39. Seasonal transfer of horses from Mérens, in the Frau gorge.

40-41. Seasonal transfer of horses from Mérens, in the high mountains of the Ariège.

42. The castle of Usson.

Horses of Mérens
Splendid vital blackness, with a white blaze and eyes full of light. Bold animals, fit for a noble, frontierless land. A multitude of eyes and hooves all moving towards a common goal. Man can only follow.

Usson
The sky, overwhelmingly blue, will be as hard as a wall against the wind. And the wind, which makes it way scattering shadows and light, will weave slumbering traces that echo the streams of the Bruyante as it flows at the foot of the walls.

Puilaurens
Nothing remains of the first castle built on this site. These ruins are what is left of the last. Castles are like human beings: they pass through childhood, adult vigour and old age to a motionless eternity - not stripped of flesh but released from the flesh, in all lights and all weathers.

H.G.

Puilaurens
Winter came. The sky turned grey. Mist surrounded the castle, and, wind-blown, seemed to stretch out the length of the walls. A light snow began to fall. This happened many centuries ago.

Pays de Sault
Here is something to confirm that man exists in more than the shadow of his memory, more than in the ruins left by his wars. All the Grand Sault speaks of peace, of flocks, of stubborn forests in mellow, protective autumn weather.

Arques
This is a northern keep set down in the heart of the south, for the castle that we see today was built in the thirteenth century by Gilles, grandson of Pierre de Voisins, a close companion in arms of Simon de Montfort. The style is that of the Kingdom of France; the stone is that of Corbières. It is a work of art, a redeeming product of a time of grief.
H.G.

Alet-les-Bains
Above, in the blue thicket of branches, in the interlacing boughs, the tower of the church struggles with transparent poplars. As you look, bear in mind the damp earth, the grasses of the fishponds, and the sugar-sweet scent at the foot of the curtain of trees.

64

65

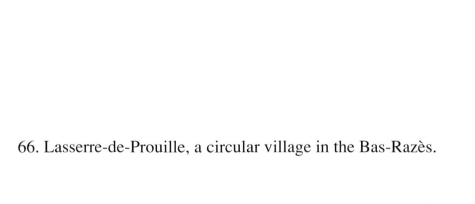

66. Lasserre-de-Prouille, a circular village in the Bas-Razès.

Carcassonne

Here, in the capital of Raymond-Roger Trencavel, viscount of Carcassonne and Béziers, a series of debates was held in 1204 on the initiative of Pedro II of Aragon. On one side were the papal legate Pierre de Castelnau and Brother Raoul; on the other, the Cathar bishop Bernard de Simorre. Some were presided over by St Dominic.

In 1209, when the crusaders arrived, Raymond-Roger strengthened the town in preference to Béziers, which was sacked and burnt. On 15 August Carcassonne was captured after a two-week siege. Trencavel was taken prisoner, and Simon de Montfort received the title of viscount of Carcassonne and Béziers.

After Simon's death in 1218 the title passed to his son Amaury. In 1224, the town was recaptured by Raymond Trencavel, son of Raymond-Roger. In 1225 there is mention of a Cathar bishop; but in 1226 the population, terrified by the arrival of the royal army, expelled their new viscount, and Louis VIII installed his seneschal, Humbert de Beaujeu.

In September 1240 Trencavel besieged the town again, but withdrew on the arrival of a royal army.

The walled town was substantially rebuilt and enlarged by Philippe le Bel and then restored by Viollet-le-Duc in the mid-nineteenth century. During the past twenty years, the slate roofs erected at that time have been gradually replaced by terracotta tiles.

Carcassonne
Proud, arrogant even, and yet moving in its mantle of ramparts. These walls have heard the voice of Simon de Montfort and that of Trencavel, who with his five hundred riders mounted on Arab horses tried for a moment to defy the twenty thousand crusaders sent against him from Narbonne. Every cranny in the masonry shelters invisible beings, fragments of history, lives. Too often seen, perhaps, and too well known - yet Carcassonne remains a secret wonder.

                                                                    H.G.

ON THE FOLLOWING PAGES

80. A cherry-tree in blossom beside the Argent-Double river.

81. La Tourette Cabardès: octagonal tower of the church of Ste-Anne, twelfth century.

82. Mas Cabardès: the weavers' cross.

83. Miraval Cabardès: painted door of a house.

84. Montréal: the village, crowned by the Collégiale or collegiate church.

85. Bram, a village built in a circle around the church.

86. Fields of oilseed rape near Fanjeaux.

87-89. The Lauragais, rich in many different crops.

90. Vineyards under snow in the Razès region.

Lastours

There are four castles on these rocks: Cabaret, Quertinheux, Tour-Régine (a royal fortress built after the crusade), and Fleur-Espine, with its name that sounds like the innocent heroine of an old tale.
Here dwelt some of the fiercest opponents of the invading crusaders. The men and the times were equally savage; but their lives were lived closer to heaven than ours.

H.G.

Citou

The ruins crowning the rock seem formed by a single storm. Slender and simple, almost emaciated, like the blade of an axe, they press forward above the valley with the manifest intention of splitting it apart so that a stream may always run through it.

At Fanjeaux stood an important stronghold of the count of Toulouse. Simon de Montfort occupied it in 1205-6, and in 1209 the count of Foix attempted to recapture it from the crusaders. Like Lavaur, Termes and Minerve, the castle was an intellectual centre that suffered greatly from the crusade. Fanjeaux was also an active centre of Catharism: in 1223, the Cathar bishop Guilhabert de Castres was recorded as having owned a house and a hospice for over thirty years, and another mention ten years later shows him still involved with the place.

St Dominic and the bishop of Osma at the outset of their preaching careers challenged the Cathars in debates, an exercise much favoured at the time. A Dominican house was then established, at Prouille, to provide a refuge for Cathar women who had converted to orthodox Christianity. The Dominican Order of Preaching Friars was recognized by the pope in 1218.

O Holy Father
Just God of all virtuous spirits
See
how time, the last mason of your house
has finished his work
and goes on his way.

At the fountain of the orchard
by the pebbles in the green grass
in the shade of a fruit tree
flowers of the morning all presented
songs of birds among the leaves
I met in solitude
she who keeps my wound unhealed.

MARCABRUN
translated by Henri Gougaud.

87 88

89 90

Toulouse is the most mysterious of cities - rose-pink and rough, old and yet strong, open and reserved, mystical no less than rebellious. At the foot of its walls Simon de Montfort died, struck down by a missile fired by women. In front of the church of St-Etienne many heretics were burnt, and St-Sernin was the scene of naive miracles before silence was cultivated in the cloister of the Jacobins, the secret heart of the city. Around that now is nothing but memory and the sound of time.

H.G.

Ah ! Toulouse and Provence
and the land of Argence,
Carcassonne and Béziers
I saw and see you still !

SICARD DE MARVEJOLS
translated by Henri Gougaud.

Toulouse

Capital of an immense county whose lords in the twelfth century vied with the Trencavels, Toulouse was governed after 1189 by a commune headed by consuls. It was an intellectual centre where the philosophy of Aristotle was taught long before the foundation of the university in 1229. The inhabitants showed Cathar leanings from an early date: in 1167 the Bulgarian bishop Nicetas organized a Cathar council at St-Felix de Caraman, near Toulouse. Raymond V was already thinking of suppressing the movement.

In 1211 negotiations between Raymond VI and the papal legates collapsed and hostilities immediately broke out. Simon de Montfort entered the territory of Toulouse after the bonfire of Cassès, where sixty heretics were burnt, taking advantage of the violent opposition between the count and Bishop Foulque, a former troubadour, who was determined to restore the power of the Church. Simon besieged the city, but soon gave up for lack of means. In 1213 Pedro II of Aragon, appointed as a mediator, was welcomed in by the citizens. Simon de Montfort, entrenched in the castle of Muret, fought and won the battle of Muret in which Pedro II was killed. In 1215 the crusaders' leader was placed in charge of Toulouse and the future Louis VIII made his ceremonial entrance.

In 1216, although Simon de Montfort had begun to dismantle the walls and to strengthen the Château Narbonnais to serve as his own headquarters, Raymond, the son of Raymond VI, made his entry as a liberator. Simon, checked at Beaucaire, marched on Toulouse: a popular rising was crushed and the city was again laid waste.

But it was not defeated. In 1217 Simon had to embark on a third siege, and during it he was killed. The crusaders withdrew. The city had triumphed. In 1219, it was the future Louis VIII's turn to be thwarted.

The treaty of Meaux in 1229, however, put an end to the crusade. Raymond VII agreed to dismantle the fortifications of Toulouse and to marry his daughter to a son of Louis VIII, Alphonse de Poitiers. As a sign of his submission, he was beaten with rods at Notre-Dame in Paris by the cardinal legate on Maundy Thursday. The commissioners of the regent, Blanche of Castile, officially took possession of the city, and a university was founded.

Even then, resistance was not dead: in 1235 the population rose up against the Inquisitors and the Dominicans. On the death of Alphonse de Poitiers in 1271 the city finally lost its independence.

For a long time, construction work on the cathedral took second place to the building of the church of the Jacobins. The nave was paid for by Raymond VI, but the present choir was not begun until the episcopacy of Bertrand de l'Ile-Jourdain (1272-86). When he died it was still unfinished, and it was only in 1609, after a fire, that the timber roof of the choir was replaced by a stone vault.

The church of the Jacobins

The Dominican house in Toulouse was founded in 1215. Construction of the church began before the monastic buildings in 1260; in 1285 the apse vault was completed, and in 1292 the first mass was celebrated.

The church of the Jacobins was the church of the university, which was a major centre of anti-Cathar preaching. The importance of its intellectual role was recognized by the translation here of the relics of St Thomas Aquinas, the great thirteenth-century Dominican friar and learned theologian. The church originally had a belltower, which was demolished in 1795.

Albi Cathedral

The present cathedral is essentially a post-crusade building. In 1277 the Dominican Bernard de Castanet, newly appointed bishop and Inquisitor, decided to begin rebuilding his church. The old cathedral was not immediately destroyed, however, since the foundations of the new one were laid alongside, and it was not until the end of the fourteenth century that Bishop Dominique de Florence had all of the old work swept away except for the Roman cloister, which itself disappeared a century later.

In keeping with the idea of spiritual reconquest, by force if necessary, Bernard de Castanet constructed his church as a fortress. With the troubled times of the fourteenth century and the threat of undisciplined mercenary armies, that character was intensified.

The upper parts of the building were altered in the nineteenth century during restoration work by César Daly, though many of his alterations have now been removed.

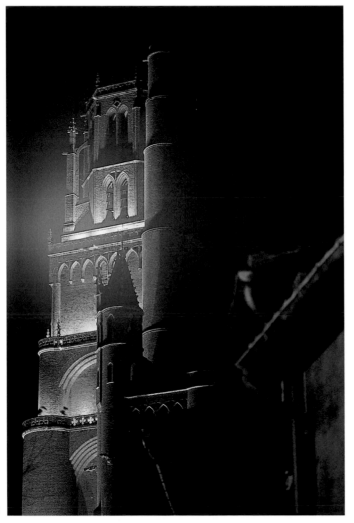

Minerve

Here one hundred and forty heretics died. Made prisoners after an agonizing battle in full armour in the blazing heat of July, their bodies perished but their souls did not yield. None renounced his faith. They marched to the stake amid the crosses and banners of the victors, convinced against all reason that they would never die.

H.G.

It was a natural defence that was said to be impregnable. In 1210 Simon de Montfort exploited the hostility between Guillaume, viscount of Minerve, and the inhabitants of the Narbonne region to win over the loyalty of the latter, and in June 1210 the fortress fell after a four-month siege. Minerve saw the first great bonfire of heretics: one hundred and forty were captured and burnt. During the revolt of 1240, Minerve opened its gates to the occitan lords supporting Raymond Trencavel.

Béziers

The sack of Béziers on 22 July 1209, the feast day of St Mary Magdalen, placed the seal of atrocity on the beginning of the Albigensian crusade. The town was wealthy, administered by consuls who owed allegiance to the bishop and the viscount; and it was also turbulent. In 1161 the inhabitants killed the former and attacked the latter in the church of the Madeleine. It was an intellectual town where heresy was rife. St Dominic organized debates and preached, but with little effect.

In 1209 Raymond-Roger Trencavel, viscount of Carcassonne and Béziers, found himself faced with the crusaders marching on Carcassonne and decided to strengthen the citadel there, leaving the defence of Béziers to the consuls. On 21 July Bishop Reynaud de Montpeyroux, who had succeeded the murdered Guillaume de Roquessels, tried to negotiate a settlement: the town would be spared if

222 named heretics were handed over. The citizens refused either to do that or to surrender.

The next day, the crusaders took advantage of an ill-advised sortie by the defenders to enter the town, and the inhabitants took refuge in the cathedral of St-Nazaire and the churches of St-Jude and Ste-Madeleine. What followed was a general massacre. "Kill them all; God will recognize his own" - such was the verdict of the papal legate Arnaud Amaury, abbot of Cîteaux, according to the German chronicler Cesaire of Herstenbach. Simon de Montfort became viscount of Béziers and Carcassonne. The town recovered rapidly. In 1224 Raymond Trencavel, the son of Raymond-Roger, regained the title of viscount. But two years later, Louis VIII set out on crusade and marched against the town, which immediately declared its loyalty to the Crown, and was occupied by the king.

It was in a council at Béziers in 1243 that the bishops of the Languedoc took the decision to deal once and for all with Montségur.

Béziers
In this rock the colour of sickly flesh there remains the memory of a ghastly river without water. Nothing but men and weapons, nothing but the insane fire of faith. Thousands of bodies in a single terrifying stream.

Fontfroide

The Cistercian house of Fontfroide was one of the most important abbeys in the Languedoc, and like Granselve it was the centre of an intense spiritual life; here the troubadour Foulque de Marseille (later bishop of Toulouse) took his vows as a monk. Fontfroide had some incidental links with the crusade. Pierre de Castelnau, archdeacon of Maguelonne and papal legate in Languedoc, was a Cistercian from this community; and it was his assassination in 1208 at St-Gilles by an officer of Raymond VI, count of Toulouse, that provided the pretext for the launching of the crusade. In 1204, with another monk of Fontfroide, Brother Raoul, Pierre de Castelnau had organized public debates in Carcassonne in the presence of Pedro II of Aragon, where thirteen Christians and thirteen Cathars served as judges.
On his death in 1225 Arnaud Amaury, archbishop of Narbonne, who had played a major role in the crusade, bequeathed to the abbey his books, his weapons and his war-horse.

Villerouge-Termenès

Here Bélibaste, the last of the Cathar Perfecti, was burnt. This simple village was the setting for the final act of the whole cruel and magnificent saga. Every summer, now, that time is commemorated - not lamented but reenacted, celebrated, as if reviving the inextinguishable desire for happiness and transforming those old wounds into paths of discovery.

H.G.

Termes

From the top of these walls, Raymond de Termes shouted his defiance at Simon de Montfort's crusaders caught in the quagmires down in the valley. Raymond thought himself impregnable, but he was defeated. Not so his land. That is still unconquered today - the wild silence of the garrigues and the humble, proud peace of a region which is left unchallenged to birds, elusive animals, and the scent of herbs.

H.G.

I know a kingdom where no king lives,
I know counties without a lord,
I know marches where no marquis rules,
powerful castles, fine dwellings -
but the castle-dwellers are there no more.

BERTRAND DE BORN
translated by Henri Gougaud.

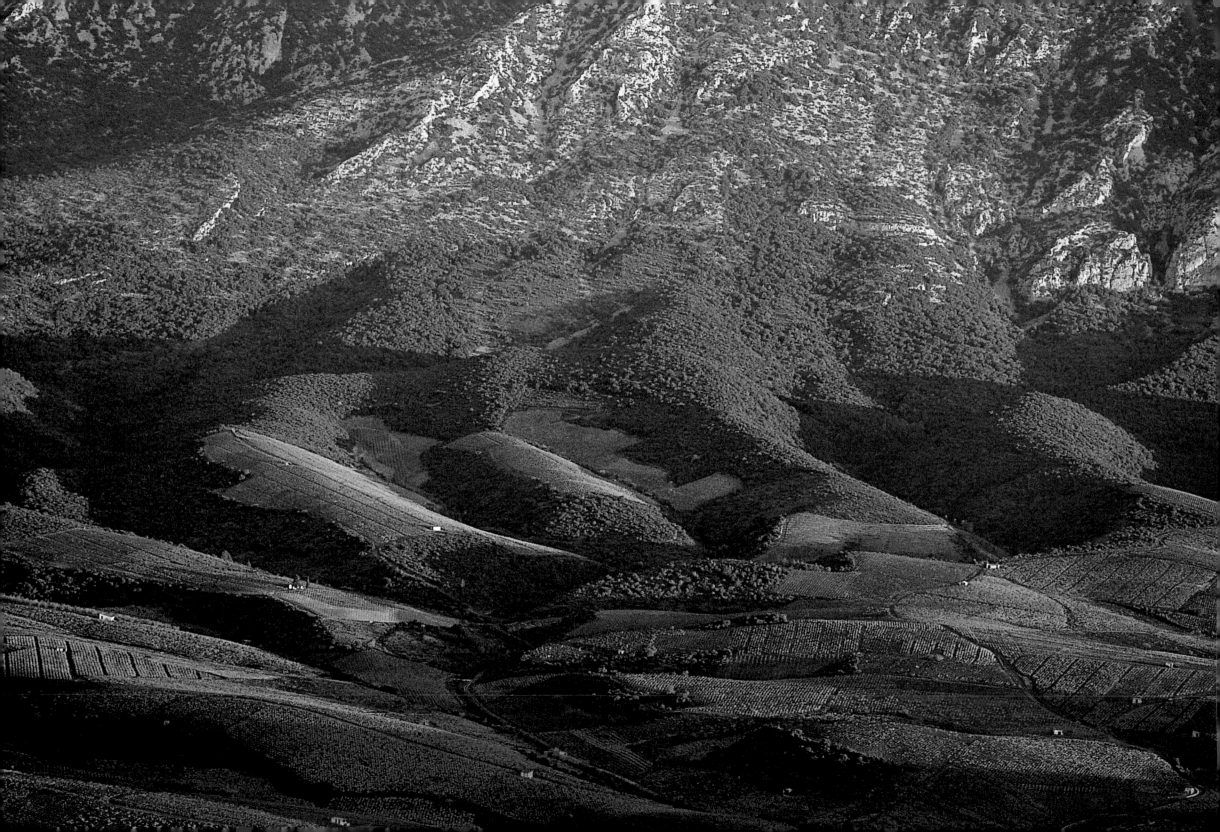

Peyrepertuse
High in the rocky sky, like a ship with its prow rearing up, Peyrepertuse seems to defy the boldest of human enterprises. In fact it capitulated after a miserable three-day siege, its souls, not its stones, undermined.

H.G.

Peyrepertuse is an enormous citadel that covers 7,000 square metres. Invested unsuccessfully by the troops of Simon de Montfort in 1216, in 1240 it was captured by the royal army after a siege of a few days. St Louis perfected the fortifications and built a second castle to the west, on the Roc St-Jordy. Structures surviving from the twelfth century are the old keep, transformed into a cistern, and a small circuit of walls.

Quéribus
The wind is always clean and always fierce around this stone fist clenched at the sky. Long after the time of the Cathars, Quéribus was a stronghold of brigands. Now nothing comes to trouble the abandoned citadel, which has humbly learned to reckon its weight in dust.

H.G.

Situated at the top of a cliff 800 metres high, Quéribus was held to be invincible, and indeed it only surrendered very late, in 1255. At the centre of the fortress is a room created in the fourteenth century where eight rib vaults spring from a single pillar.

Aguilar

There are times when from Aguilar there seems to spring the immense trunk of a tree of light with invisible leaves, a transparent fountain, a shimmering velvet stream with all the colours of the rainbow, issuing from a grey fist whose force is spent.

WORKS PUBLISHED
UNDER THE AEGIS OF THE PAYS CATHARE

Le Sentier Cathare, de la mer à Montségur, by Mireille Barthes, Dominique Baudreu, Nicolas Gouzy, Louis Salavy and Jean-Pierre Sarret (3rd edn, Tarbes/Carcassonne, Randonnées pyrénéennes, Comité de Randonnées de l'Aude, 1991).

Carcassonne et le Pays Cathare, Guide Bleu (Paris, Hachette, 1991).

Hérésis, a journal devoted to the study of medieval heresy, which publishes research and editions of texts (11600 Villegly, Centre National d'Etudes Cathares, Centre René Nelli, 1983).

Monographs published by the Centre d'Archéologie médiévale du Languedoc and the Comité départemental du patrimoine culturel audois (one monograph per building, site or topic):
Châteaux médiévaux du Languedoc (on medieval castles): *Aguilar, Arques, Châteaux médiévaux de l'Aude, Lastours, Montségur, Peyrepertuse, Puilaurens, Puivert, Quéribus, Termes, Villerouge-Termenès*.
Abbayes médiévales du Languedoc (on medieval abbeys): *Alet, Caunes, Fontfroide, Lagrasse, St-Hilaire, St-Papoul*.
Cités médiévales du Languedoc (on medieval fortified towns): *Carcassonne, Minerve*.

Ombre et lumière du Pays Cathare, by Michel Roquebert and Catherine Bibolet (Toulouse, Privat, 1992).

Vivre le Pays Cathare, by Gérard Sioen and Henri Gougaud (Paris, Mengès, 1992).

Découvrir le Pays Cathare, by Michèle Aue (Vic-en-Bigorre, M.S.M., 1992).